MW01503682

The Philosophy of Bitcoin

The Philosophy of Bitcoin

Álvaro D. María

Bitcoin Magazine Books
Nashville, TN

Published by Bitcoin Magazine Books
An imprint of BTC Media, LLC
438 Houston St. #257 Nashville, TN 37203
Address all inquiries to:
contact@btcmedia.org

Cover art: Miraggio
Originally translated by: Aurora González Sanz
Formatting by RMK Publications, LLC

For my grandmother,

for being an example of generosity.

Table of Contents

PART 3

[…]
For a trifle more or less
All his power will confess,
Over kings and priests and scholars
Rules the mighty Lord of Dollars.

[…]
And the ugliest at his side
Shines with all of beauty's pride;
Over kings and priests awl scholars
Rules the mighty Lord of Dollars.

He's a gallant, he's a winner,
Black or white be his complexion;
He is brave without correction
As a Moor or Christian sinner.
He makes cross and medal bright,
And he smashes laws of right, —
Over kings and priests and scholars
Rules the mighty Lord of Dollars.

Noble are his proud ancestors
For his blood-veins are patrician;
Royalties make the position
Of his Orient investors;
So they find themselves preferred
To the duke or country herd, —
Over kings and priests and scholars,
Rules the mighty Lord of Dollars!

Of his standing who can question
When there yields unto his rank, a
Hight-Castillian Doña Blanca,
If you follow the suggestion? —
He that crowns the lowest stool,
And to hero turns the fool, —
Over kings and priests and scholars,
Rules the mighty Lord of Dollars.

On his shields are noble bearings;
His emblazonments unfurling
Show his arms of royal sterling
All his high pretensions airing;
And the credit of his miner
Stands behind the proud refiner,
Over kings and priests and scholars
Rules the mighty Lord of Dollars.

Contracts, bonds, and bills to render,
Like his counsels most excelling,
Are esteemed within the dwelling
Of the banker and the lender.
So is prudence overthrown,
And the judge complaisant grown, —
Over kings and priests and scholars
Rules the mighty Lord of Dollars.

Such indeed his sovereign standing
(With some discount in the order),
Spite the tax, the cash-recorder
Still his value fixed is branding.
He keeps rank significant
To the prince or finn in want,—
Over kings and Priests and scholars
Rules the mighty Lord of Dollars.

Never meets he dames ungracious
To his smiles or his attention,
How they glow but at the mention
Of his promises capacious!
And how bare-faced they become
To the coin beneath his thumb
Over kings and Priests and scholars
Rules the mighty Lord of Dollars.

Mightier in peaceful season
(And in this his wisdom showeth)
Are his standards, than when bloweth
War his haughty blasts and breeze on;
In all foreign lands at home,
Equal e'en in pauper's loam,—
Over kings and priests and scholars
Rules the mighty Lord of Dollars.

—Quevedo on #Bitcoin[i]

---

[i] Translation by Thomas Walsh.

Foreword

The Philosophy of Bitcoin

Why This Book Matters

Multiple global crises are besieging our everyday lives. Pandemics, war, inflation, economic decline, and recession seem to have come out of nowhere. Even more baffling are the responses from our leaders to these problems: lockdowns, forced vaccination, health passports, price controls, increased financial surveillance, public fear campaigns, and the spread of fake news.

Are these events connected? Are they the visible symptoms of much deeper, behind-the-scenes developments?

This book is an invitation to explore the structural changes happening in our global society. It is also an exposé of how the economic and political paradigms we know are becoming obsolete and why brave philosophical disruption may offer us hope to build a better society.

Following the multidisciplinary approach of Ancient Greece, where the arts, mathematics, philosophy, and political science were boldly analyzed and debated, Álvaro D. María takes us on a journey through all the dimensions in which Bitcoin will transform our institutions, governments, and lives, beyond the technological and economic perspectives.

This book presents a deep yet concise explanation of why these are pivotal times that will change our society in ways unimaginable even one decade ago. Using a rigorous historical perspective, Álvaro demystifies money, authority, and power to help us understand how the development of Bitcoin may unshackle money from the chains held by national states.

The Philosophy of Bitcoin dares the reader to suspect the status quo, to deconstruct fundamental paradigms about government funding, and political structures that have been hidden from public opinion by the media and academia for decades, and to question why our societies are shaped the way they are, so that we can devise possible alternatives.

The discovery (and I use "discovery" rather than "invention" advisedly) of Bitcoin gave birth to a new Internet era that incorporates a native open financial system. In this sense, this book explains how Bitcoin redefines property rights and makes state violence less effective upon freer citizens. This new reality will most probably challenge government tax collection and the funding of old, nation-state structures. The author also discusses the positive regulatory competition among nation-states that may arise from the different paces at which countries understand these phenomena. Governments with large fiscal deficits and economies based on agro-industrial structures might try to fight Bitcoin's financial innovation in order to preserve strict control over their private productive sectors. On the other hand, technology-based economies could see an opportunity to simplify their respective social contracts to retain and attract global digital talent. These are but two examples of the wealth of ideas and itineraries that the reader can follow to enter the conceptual realm of Bitcoin, often perceived as elusive or unintelligible.

The repertoire of questions we are inspired to reflect upon is equally rich. Which public services should be provided by governments in the future? What should a fair taxation level be? The reader will find these discussions essential to the future of our global society; far from providing a unified solution, Bitcoin may stimulate open competition between national states with different public services and tax structures and even change the balance of power in favor of the people, leading to the development of new types of social contracts following the ideas of John Locke.

In this respect, the final section of *The Philosophy of Bitcoin* is enlightening for politicians navigating these uncharted courses. Every disruptive technological innovation presents risks and opportunities. In an environment of unsustainable national debt levels and debasing *fiat* currencies, short-sighted politicians might find that Bitcoin exposes them to social accountability as it hinders the funding of their budgetary needs through inflationary tax. However, as Álvaro clearly explains, opposition to Bitcoin adoption could become the last fatal error of governments trying to hold onto a sinking legacy financial system.

This book is an open invitation to everyone to think about the future of money and State. Should these two institutions inevitably be connected? Should money be backed by authority or by scarcity? Can a separation of money and State bring benefits to the societies of the future? What types of national states would perform better in this possible scenario? Are we starting to witness major changes in the social contract between empowered free individuals and governments?

About the Timing of This Book

The timing of a particular event may be as important as the event itself. The Bitcoin white paper was published during the 2008 Global Crisis. While the real estate speculative bubble, created by decades of cumulative expansion of the monetary base and low interest rates, was blowing up, Satoshi Nakamoto presented to the world the first decentralized, scarce digital asset that ever existed. Today, almost fifteen years later, we are witnessing another critical moment in history. With major economies eroded by high inflation, unsustainable debt-to-GDP ratios, widening inequality, and rising social unrest, the cracks in the Bretton Woods system are becoming evident to a larger audience.

In this regard, the timing of *The Philosophy of Bitcoin* is impeccable. After a decade and a half, Bitcoin has overcome attacks and censorship attempts while enabling scaling solutions through the development of upper layers on top of it. Bitcoin has over a hundred million users; furthermore, one country, El Salvador, has already implemented it as legal global tender. Such a network effect makes it possible to foresee Bitcoin as the potential base layer of the financial system of the future: an uncensorable, neutral global store of value, as well as a permission-less open monetary network to exchange value across the globe (and beyond). We are now freer individuals as Bitcoin provides us with a new digital financial system that protects the private property And privacy of the people, while upholding trust through immutable code. As a result, this is the right time to start thinking about the philosophical and political implications that the falling of the *fiat* system and the mass adoption of Bitcoin could have in the future of our society.

Call for Action

What kind of society we will inhabit in the next decades is yet to be defined—or decided. This book invites the reader to react, to understand the changes we are living through, to contribute to the construction of future nation-states, decentralized communities and even micropolises (more on this in Álvaro's next book), to put the power of government back in the hands of the people and repair a social fabric unraveled by more than fifty years of *fiat* money.

Hobbes's Leviathan has gone rogue and, for the first time in human history, we have the technological tools to put it back in its place, to provide protection and safety to free individuals. We can use Bitcoin technology in a new, post–national-state era to bring as much social well-being, peace, and prosperity as possible to all humankind.

Gabriel Kurman

March, 2023

Preface

There is nothing more practical than a good theory.

Kurt Lewin on #Bitcoin

This book has a dual purpose: to provoke a crisis about two widely held beliefs. The first is that a currency that is money must be backed by an authority. The second, that the "State" is a concept that can be applied to any political society and it is not possible to think of post-State political forms.

It has always seemed to me that more philosophers are needed when it comes to thinking about economics. Certainly, it seems difficult to understand the need for this statement. After all, the philosopher who has dealt most with economic issues is Karl Marx, a man who left a series of brilliant contributions; among them that of reminding us that economics is always political economy, and such a terrible influence in the world that anyone would dare to say that philosophers have to dedicate themselves to making *Philosophy of Economics* after the twentieth century. However, economics as a discipline lacks reflections on the analyses it carries out in its field. Normally, these reflections on the analyses are made by economists themselves, who rarely have training in fields such as politics and philosophy. Sometimes they have some legal education, but generally, they try to apply the conclusions of their analyses to political societies thinking economics is a science, and something that depends on politics. As Marx reminded us, economics can hardly reach such a status of science, so when they speak of economics as a science, they are unknowingly doing philosophy, a substitute in which they give their vision of the world based on the conclusions of the analyses of their field.

I have devoted most of my study to the theory of the State and the philosophy of law, and secondarily I have tried to study economic issues, especially monetary ones. Interestingly, my analyses concluded that we were facing the crisis of the State, an inevitable crisis, since the dynamics that govern them following their principles, make it impossible both to reform the State towards other political forms and to oppose it since it leaves almost no room to do anything against it. Moreover, the State have no qualms about going all out to attack anyone who dares to challenge them, so any attack seemed doomed to fail, despite we were clearly facing an exhausted political form. My conclusion was then that the only form of political action against the State must be *cryptocratic,* one in which the State could do nothing because it did not know who was behind the attacks against it. However, I could not think of any way in which this could be developed, I did not even see the possible environment for its development. Well, *cyberspace* is that space, and Bitcoin its best weapon.

Writing in Davos, Switzerland on February 8, 1996, John Perry Barlow [1] issued the following manifesto:

A Declaration of the Independence of Cyberspace

Governments of the Industrial World, you weary giants of flesh and steel, I come from Cyberspace, the new home of Mind. On behalf of the future, I ask you of the past to leave us alone. You are not welcome among us. You have no sovereignty where we gather.

We have no elected government, nor are we likely to have one, so I address you with no greater authority than that with which liberty itself always speaks. I declare the global social space we are building to be naturally independent of the tyrannies you seek to impose on us. You have no moral right to rule us *nor do you possess any methods of enforcement* we have true reason to fear.

Governments derive their just powers from the consent of the governed. You have neither solicited nor received ours. We did not invite you. You do not know us, nor do you know our world. Cyberspace does not lie within your borders. Do not think that you can build it, as though it were a public construction project. You cannot. It is an act of nature and it grows itself through our collective actions.

You have not engaged in our great and gathering conversation, nor did you create the wealth of our marketplaces. You do not know our culture, our ethics, or the unwritten codes that already provide our society more order than could be obtained by any of your impositions.

You claim there are problems among us that you need to solve. You use this claim as an excuse to invade our precincts. Many of these problems don't exist. Where there are real conflicts, where there are wrongs, we will identify them and address them by our means. We are forming our own Social Contract. This governance will arise according to the conditions of our world, not yours. Our world is different.

Cyberspace consists of transactions, relationships, and thought itself, arrayed like a standing wave in the web of our communications. Ours is a world that is both everywhere and nowhere, but it is not where bodies live.

We are creating a world that *all may enter* without privilege or prejudice accorded by race, economic power, military force, or station of birth.

We are creating a world where anyone, anywhere may express his or her beliefs, no matter how singular, without fear of being coerced into silence or conformity.

Your legal concepts of *property*, expression, identity, movement, and context do not apply to us. They are all based on matter, and there is no matter here.

Our identities have no bodies, so, unlike you, we cannot obtain order by physical coercion. […]

You are terrified of your own children, since they are natives in a world where you will always be immigrants. *Because you fear them, you entrust your bureaucracies with the parental responsibilities you are too cowardly to confront yourselves.* In our world, all the sentiments and expressions of humanity, from the debasing to the angelic, are parts of a seamless whole, the global conversation of bits. We cannot separate the air that chokes from the air upon which wings beat. […]

We must declare our virtual selves immune to your *sovereignly*, even as we continue to consent to your rule over our bodies. We will spread ourselves across the planet so that no one can arrest our thoughts.

We will create a civilization of the Mind in Cyberspace. May it be more humane and fairer than the world your governments have made before.

Madrid, Spain. May 16, 2021, Álvaro D. María

Introduction

"Crisis" means judgment, but a decisive judgment (from the Greek verb, *krino*), revisory and selective, implying a re-judging of the usual criteria, a judgment of the judgment. The usual judgment constitutes a state of opinion, the established estimates, the ideas in circulation. The two fundamental products of that usual estimation, in circulation, are: on the one hand, currency, and, on the other hand, the law. That both currency and the law have suffered in our days' inflation, a devaluation, in short, a loss of prestige, is a fact that is plain to see. It should not be forgotten, however, that the crisis of currency and the crisis of the law are but two evidential aspects of the same phenomenon: *the radical crisis of the modern world.* Hence the seriousness and topicality of the subject.

"Romanists Facing the Current Crisis of Law"
Álvaro d'Ors on #Bitcoin

The status quo is to be constituted by those beliefs that are in the environment in which we develop. These beliefs are part of us in an intimate, and at the same time, communitarian way, they are there without us being aware of them. We assimilate them by osmosis of our historical circumstances, and they are so evident to us that we will not admit a different thought or an occurrence opposed to them. They construct us as subjects because we are sustained by them. It is through them that we interpret reality and, as Ortega rightly pointed out, they are of a different nature than ideas.

On certain occasions, obstacles appear in our lives that we are not able to remove with the beliefs that sustain us, and we need a new tool to be able to deal with the problem we are facing. When our beliefs prove to be insufficient to give an answer, they regain their status as historical ideas, but as beliefs are the ground on which we tread, we find ourselves as if in an abyss— as if an earthquake has opened a crack in the ground under our feet. Like those beliefs, we find ourselves in doubt—not on firm ground, but on the sea after a shipwreck. This is a crisis, and it is here that we must make a judgment on new developments and decide where to continue in the course of history.

Well, two beliefs are falling into a crisis and it is up to us to decide where to continue. These beliefs are that a currency that is money must have the backing of the authority and that the "State" is a concept that can be applied to any political society and it is not possible to think of post-State political forms. In short, the crisis of the State and the present currency.

In our time, at least in the Western world, previous epochs— with their wars, famines, hyperinflation and pandemics—were looked down upon as a time when humanity was still underage, undemocratic, and unscientific. However, COVID-19, widespread rearmament, demographic imbalances, currency expansions, and escalating small conflicts are beginning to generate some nervousness.

There was as little belief in the possibility of such barbaric declines as wars between the peoples of Europe as there was in witches and ghosts. Our fathers were comfortably saturated with confidence in the unfailing and binding power of tolerance and conciliation. [...] It is reasonable that we, who have long since struck the word "security" from our vocabulary as a myth, should smile at the optimistic delusion of that idealistically blinded generation [...] We of the new generation who have learned not to be surprised by any outbreak of bestiality, we who each new day expect things worse than the day before, are markedly more skeptical about a possible moral improvement of mankind. We must agree with Freud, to whom our culture and civilization were merely a thin layer liable at any moment to be pierced by the destructive forces of the 'underworld.' [...] that world of security was naught but a castle of dreams; my parents lived in it as if it had been a house of stone.[2]

The World of Yesterday, Stefan Zweig

Part 1

The Philosophical Principles of Bitcoin

Chapter 1

The Philosophy of Money

> There is no denying that views on money are as difficult
> to describe as are shifting clouds.
>
> *History of Economic Analysis*, Schumpeter on #Bitcoin

There is no doubt that money is essential in our world. I am
not saying that it is the most important thing, simply that
it runs through our lives and is a large part of our daily
actions. It controls and moves people's wills like few other
things, but what is money? Is money the same as currency?
What are the differences?

When dealing with these issues there is usually some confusion
in the terms, we move in a pre-understanding of what money
and currency are, in a belief. We use them every day, how can
we not know what they are? It is assumed, rarely explained or
theorized about. Moreover, they are used interchangeably. In a
way, currency and money are like body and soul, matter and
form. When they are linked, they could be called circulating, and

when money leaves its body, currency becomes the object of study of numismatics and not a matter for economists.[ii]

It is much better understood what money is if we see it as an adjective of certain commodities, rather than as a noun. Indeed, these commodities considered money usually have certain qualities different from others: They are not usually consumable, but they are divisible, scarce, transportable, easily sold—with a lot of liquidity—storable, and fungible. They must also facilitate quantification, be difficult to manipulate, be easy to verify, and not deteriorate with the passage of time. All these qualities are what allow these commodities to be used as a *means of exchange*, to be considered *good money*. In the end, money is a commodity whose main value is to facilitate exchanges, which is an essential function, since it reduces the costs of trading, which is why it is so fundamental in societies.

In the social imaginary, money has a certain peculiarity that makes it unique. It is a social product vilified and despised in public life, and yet there is no other social product that is sought after and desired more than money. Much ink has been used to point it out as the culprit of many of man's ills and, despite everything, it seems to be completely indifferent to it; it continues its course, knowing it is vital in society. In spite of being the object of all kinds of criticism, the existence of money has practically never been seriously questioned. There has been discussion of the death of God, of the death of Democracy, of the end of Art, of the death of Philosophy, of the decadence of

---

[ii] Hayek (Nobel Prize in Economy 1974) defended that "money" is an adjective, not a noun. A Roman coin is no longer money – yet it is still a coin (currency). When they are linked (money-currency), like body and soul, they are circulating (a dollar bill is money today). •When money leaves its body (the Roman coin is no longer used in exchanges, it is no longer money), the coin is not studied by economists, but by numismatics. •On a different note, cigars in prison are money, but they are not coins. This goes to say, they are not synonyms. The difference between these two concepts is what I analyse and study in my book.

Civilization; but money is still there, reviled for its power, its influence, and its capacity of seduction, but indispensable.

It is credited with fostering individualism by untying social ties when it is precisely the most social product of all. If you ask someone, "What would you take to a desert island if you could only take three things?" No one would choose money. In practice, money acts as a record of social exchange, of relationships with others, where it reflects the value of what was exchanged at a particular time.

Certainly, money does have reasons—maybe not justified but emotional ones—to be reviled, especially as it increasingly encompasses more and more social relations. Money makes explicit and brings to light the interests of social relations. Contrary to what is often said, like power, money does not corrupt, it betrays. It links many social relations to economic calculation. This is a problem for community life, especially for social ties since they are woven by the *sacred*, by uses and customs, by relations of tacit consent, all this is often considered of incalculable value. For this reason, money is considered to *desacralize*, which is why it will be the object of all kinds of criticism. Let's take a brief look at its evolution through currency.

Chapter 2

The Philosophy of Currency

> For in every country of the world, I believe, the avarice and injustice of princes and sovereign states, abusing the confidence of their subjects, have by degrees diminished the real quantity of metal, which had been originally contained in their coins.
>
> *The Wealth of Nations*, Adam Smith on #Bitcoin

T he origin of money is usually referred to as barter, however, there is no historical evidence that this happened.[iii] At least not for anything that could be

---

[iii] Luis Carlos Martín Jiménez explains it as follows: "Barter, understood as mere exchange, is at the level of systematic plundering, or the theft of goods or women between tribes. It is impossible that barter markets are the 'natural' factor that has given rise to currency as a 'brilliant solution that men reach to facilitate their transactions.' Actually, mercantile barter has never existed as a 'natural' way of trade. These exchanges are not deficient or have problems of quantification. There are no anthropological precedents that affirm that economic barter has existed in any human society. If we look in Greece before the coinage how trade is explained, we find the account in which Herodotus narrates the landing of goods on the beaches through which the Phoenicians pass, who return to the ship waiting for the tribes to reciprocate with other goods that will be collected if they like or satisfy what is expected. This is what was called 'silent trade'." Martín Jiménez, L. C. (2017). Filosofía de la Moneda, El Basilisco, no. 49, pp. 57–

considered trade. Before the development of currency, certain homogeneous goods were used—such as shells, metals, silver and gold, and others—to which certain magical or *sacred* qualities were attributed, since wealth is usually related to the expression of *power* and *authority.*

Well, in order to appear as such in the course of history, currency requires the development and convergence of certain techniques together with the validation of the political authority. Following Parise, its origin would not be in Lydia, as is commonly said, since what appears there are metals with legends, marks, or signs of equivalence: "Currency has a functional form of existence different from that of the heavy metal," since the change from a marked ingot to a coin as such, backed by a political authority, was not there materialized: "With the imprint, currency is an official measure of value and a guaranteed means of purchase."[3]

This historical convergence of different techniques that coincide simultaneously is clearly embodied in Ancient Greece. The development of metallurgy and the smelting of iron allowed the minting of more homogeneous monetary units, and the scale made it possible to establish the proportion between the different coins and give them a law—validating their purity—as well as the weights of products and their relationship with these coins (to this day we still weigh most of the products to see how much we have to pay).

The other innovation that appears clearly developed is the alphabetic language, which allows coins to be marked in such a way that it is the authority that validates their legality, reducing the costs of trade since it avoids having to check the purity and veracity of the coins given in each sale-purchase. The

---

88, p. 59.

development of metallurgy, the balance, and the alphabetic language, within the *Polis*, are the three techniques that allow the technological leap and the revolution that coins represent in the course of economic history. Greece places the *agora*, the marketplace, at the center, and the fruits of that civilization are known to all.

A characteristic feature of any technique is that it is *destructive* of what it replaces, and such destruction is proportional to the level of innovation that such techniques present—just ask the Luddites—and the first thing that these coins did was to do away with all the other commodities that were previously used in exchanges, precisely those that had a magical, *sacred* character. *The* desacralizing secularizing—character of money is present from its very origin.

Thus, the new money that appears in Greece, the coin, is a more divisible, more quantifiable, more formal, more abstract money. These attributes allow us to measure and adjust with greater precision the value of goods, facilitating and increasing trade. It is imposed on others by these qualities and, being issued by the *Power*, it is not partial, it does not belong to one individual against another, it can be used by all citizens equally, and for this reason, it can totalize the whole territory it covers.

Like languages, coins have accompanied political communities and have had a greater presence when they had greater power and extension, especially in empires. From the tetradrachm of Alexander's time to the dollar as the paper money of the United States, the currency of the dominant empire has been the most influential currency. Competition between different political powers and their currencies is an essential part of the political economy. An economy where its politicization lies in the fact that most of the exchange of goods takes place through territories, and these are always under some kind of government that interferes in some way in trade, even if merely to protect it, is traversed by political decision. And historically, governments have imposed their currency, owned and issued by them in their territories. Mainly because of the need to collect taxes and to pay soldiers.

In 2023, the field of political economy has reached a global scale, both on a productive and financial level. However, currencies are mainly state-owned (or state groupings) and still bear the imprint of political authority, *we believe* it is inevitable that this should be the case. But has there been monetary innovation in the last 2,000 years?

Well, just as in Ancient Greece, in our time, a series of circumstances have arisen linked to the development of new technologies that have made possible, for the first time in monetary history, a series of very significant innovations: First, we do not need to depend on a third party to issue a currency, allowing access to anyone who so wishes and has internet access; we can design a digital currency with very good monetary qualities, making a universal and immutable public record of transactions; and many other novelties which I will develop in the following chapters.

The internet, globalization, telecommunications and computing —cyberspace—have allowed the development of Bitcoin, and, since the *destruction* of what it replaces is inherent to technological innovation, these innovations must have a destructive character proportional to its magnitude.

Chapter 3

The Denationalization of Money?

The further pursuit of the suggestion that government should
be deprived of its monopoly of the issue of money opened the
most fascinating theoretical vistas and showed the possibility
of arrangements which have never been considered. As soon as
one succeeds in freeing oneself of *the universally but tacitly
accepted creed* that a country must be supplied by its
government with its own distinctive and exclusive currency, all
sorts of interesting questions arise which have never been
examined. The result was a foray into a wholly unexplored
field.

The Denationalisation of Money, Friedrich Hayek on #Bitcoin

Hayek was writing his life's work, *Law, Legislation and
Liberty,* when suddenly something dawned on him,

which is why he interrupted the work he was doing to write, *The Denationalisation of Money*. What he realized was, no more and no less, why money should have to be issued by the government if after all, it is nothing more than another commodity with specific qualities; it could also be offered by the market. The first time I read it, it seemed like a very reasonable idea, and I even related it to the possibility that Bitcoin might be along those lines, but I didn't quite believe it. Three years later, I reread the book and gave it a second chance, and from that moment on, I also realized that this was perfectly possible, since, as Hayek says, we only need: "A money that solves the simplest problem, to stop *inflation* [...] preventing government from concealing *depreciation*."

As we have seen, coins were guaranteed by the corresponding authority, to ensure the weight and purity of currency and avoid transaction costs. However, over the centuries, the belief spread that it was the government that conferred value on money, especially after 1971, the year in which Nixon abolished the gold standard. Yes, until not so long ago, much of the money in circulation was convertible into gold. Its natural scarcity acted as a straitjacket for the political-banking power, which could not issue more paper money than the gold it had backing it.

Monetary history is the story of how governments have defrauded their citizens in the task of giving them good money. When it has not been by expressly abusing the trust they gave them, it has been through incompetence. Moreover, when there was any limit to their ability to manipulate currency, they skipped it, even going as far as confiscating gold, as Roosevelt decreed in 1933 with Executive Order 6102. If this has happened in the United States, a country that presumes to respect private property, the monetary history of the rest of the world does not leave much to be desired either.

With a little historical perspective, a few thousand years, perhaps we could have realized—like Hayek—that it was not the best idea to entrust politicians with the issuance of something as precious as money, because if we already tend to take a mile when we are given an inch, what will those who are in a position of superiority not do?

Hayek gave birth to an idea that has opened the ground under the feet of one of the most deeply rooted beliefs, it only remains to be seen if the check is mate, literally, if the sovereign has an escape:

> But since the function of government in issuing money is no longer one of merely certifying the weight and fineness of a certain piece of metal, but involves a deliberate determination of the quantity of money to be issued, governments have become wholly inadequate for the task and, it can be said without qualifications, have incessantly and everywhere abused their trust to defraud the people. [...] A government ought not, any more than a private person, to be able to take whatever it wants, but be limited strictly to the use of the means placed at its disposal by the representatives of the people, and to be unable to extend its resources beyond what the people have agreed to let it have. [...] When one studies the history of money one cannot help wondering why people should have put up for so long with governments exercising an exclusive power over 2,000 years that was regularly used to exploit and defraud them. This can be explained only by the *myth* (that the government prerogative was necessary) becoming so firmly established that it did not occur even to the professional students of these matters (for a long time including the present writer!) ever to question it. But once the validity of the established doctrine is doubted its foundation is rapidly seen to be *fragile*.[4]

Álvaro D. María

The Denationalisation of Money, Friedrich Hayek

Part 2

Bitcoin

Chapter 4

How to Approach Bitcoin?

For as the eyes of bats are to the blaze of day, so is the reason in our soul to the things which are by nature most evident of all.

Metaphysics, Book II, Aristotle on #Bitcoin

As beliefs constitute us and Bitcoin goes directly against two of the most settled and prolonged beliefs in history, the natural, instinctive reaction inevitably is to oppose it, not to believe in such an idea. It is normal, not only because there is a lot of noise and confusion around it, but because we have a predisposition to it.

As if that were not enough, Bitcoin has a huge entry barrier, and I am not referring to its price—because you can buy fractions of it, *satoshis*—nor that you have to belong to a club, get a title, or be from a particular country. On the contrary, it is an economic good of a different nature, which does not understand social classes, economic status, or race, it only requires a person wanting to access it and the internet. The barrier to entry is how extraordinarily complex it is. We are facing something multidisciplinary, of a radically different nature, and a conceptual and technological innovation. It is only comparable to revolutionary events such as currency—as we have seen—to gunpowder, which changed the configuration of armies and modified the logic of violence; or to the internet, which has meant the decentralization of production, distribution, and access to telecommunications and information globally. Therefore, it is natural to underestimate it, especially when it takes a backwards step in price, for those people who do not understand the radical change it implies or the nature it has.

I will try to show how Bitcoin is equivalent to discovering gold, but with better monetary qualities. Inventing double-entry accounting but being a global and public ledger implying a new degree of immutability and truth; while applying the internet and computer development to redefine the right of ownership by making it impossible to confiscate, universal, accessible, not dependent on third parties and unstoppable, all at the same time.

What starts as curiosity about this asset usually takes a long time to click because what it proposes is so ambitious that it is hard to believe; it seems like a simple occurrence. However, when the pieces fit together and you assimilate it, it automatically becomes an obsession, and you see the historical scope it has. It seems that there is no loose end, everything is thought out in advance; any objection you raise is already perfectly solved by mechanisms that you did not even imagine could exist more than a decade ago. In other words, approaching Bitcoin requires doing your homework, sitting down and studying it seriously. Because the first impression is that it is a thing of nerds, merely speculative, a bubble that has little to offer, that many cryptocurrencies can outperform bitcoin; that it will have some failure or can be attacked; and, especially, that if it poses any problem to the States, they will get rid of it without difficulty. I will try to answer these questions and others.

In this book, I do not intend to deal with the whole of Bitcoin, a task of dimensions that are difficult to encompass, nor even to explain its inner workings or technological innovations, fields that I do not master and about which much has already been written and developed, except those that are considered necessary. Just as reflecting on the nature of the internet, or using it, does not require knowledge of these technical and technological aspects, neither do I consider them necessary for this essay.

When Euclid presented Ptolemy with the *Elements* that the latter had asked him to write, he asked him if there was not a shorter way to learn geometry than the *Elements*, he had given him, to which Euclid replied: "There are no real ways to Geometry." This anecdote is to point out that it doesn't matter if you are the king, if you want to know geometry, you have to follow the same hard path as everyone else, which is also applicable to Bitcoin. With Bitcoin, there are no shortcuts, but once you begin to understand it, it is a dose of humility and makes you imagine a world of possibilities that were difficult to believe before. And above all, if, as everything seems to indicate, it is successful, it makes you see that there will be a transition period that is yet to be defined. Therefore, I believe that we have a moral duty, especially those who have more advantageous positions in society and the best gifted minds, to think and work on it to build a new world.

Chapter 5

What Is Bitcoin?

> I don't believe we shall ever have a good money again before
> we take the thing out of the hands of government, we can't
> take them violently out of the hands of government, all we can
> do is by some sly roundabout way introduce something that
> they can't stop.
>
> Hayek, 1984 on #Bitcoin

B itcoin clearly aspires to be that *clever introduction.* Let's see
why.

A good is only considered economic when it is scarce because if
it is not scarce, there is no reason to hoard it or exchange it, like
the air we breathe. This aspect, which is the first lesson of any
economics class, is problematic when it comes to digital goods
because they are merely data sets.

The easy thing in this digital realm is to multiply units at almost
no cost. For example, we can distribute the same image through
a messaging app to multiple people, but being able to replicate it
as many times as you want prevents it from being a scarce asset

and, therefore, worth hoarding. Moreover, for an asset that aspires to become money, its unlimited replication is tantamount to counterfeiting. Imagine that 100 monetary units from our bank could be sent to many people at once (double-spending problem).

This problem could be solved by introducing a third party to act as an intermediary and guarantee that this image or these 100 monetary units cannot be resent, as series and movies platforms or banks do with our digital currencies. But if you have to depend on a third party there are a number of considerable risks. Since you depend on their diligence, you are subject to their rules; if they have technical problems, your service is impaired; they can establish censorship mechanisms; they can be attacked; they can go bankrupt; they can be intervened by the State; etc. (*problem of the trusted third party*).

These two problems are the ones that Bitcoin manages to solve, being the first scarce digital asset that does not depend on third parties. It is a digital cash monetary system, from person to person, peer-to-peer. That is, transfers can be made between people without the need to trust another. Its supply is limited to 21 million bitcoin, although each one is divisible into 100 million *satoshis*, just as 1 *euro* can be divided into 100 *cents*. Its issuance schedule is known and immutable. Its community of users and the network that is woven around it makes it possible to issue bitcoin, trace their ownership and transfer them between individuals. In addition, it is open source, which allows a greater number of programmers to develop it and to discover its possible failures so that any technological innovation or need for improvement can also be implemented by network consensus, a decentralized network whose only concern is to secure the system and improve it.

As I have already mentioned, money is nothing more than a value registration system, Alice exchanges X with Bob and in return receives Y at O moment, while the main role of banks today—apart from financing and investment, and some policy— is to avoid double-spending of your digital money, guard your funds with fractional reserve, that is, they only keep a fraction of what their customers' deposit, and make a record of what Alice has sent to Bob at O. Well, what Bitcoin does is fulfilling that role, improving it in all aspects, and that is what I will try to develop.

Bitcoin allows you to guard your bitcoin, a currency with very good monetary qualities—as we will see, 100%, *not your keys, not your coin*. Bitcoin has a public, immutable, temporarily sealed record of all transactions that simultaneously allows you to verify the temporal order of the transactions—preventing bitcoin that have been sent before from being sent again, solving the problem of double-spending—this is the Bitcoin *blockchain*. *Blockchain* technology is an innovation comparable to double-entry accounting. Moreover, it is impossible to confiscate— redefining the right of ownership—accessible to anyone, it can't be censored and its transactions cannot be stopped by a third party. Next, we will look at all its qualities in detail and confront Bitcoin with its alternatives.

I will reproduce what we discussed earlier about the qualities of money:

> It is much better understood what money is if we see it as an adjective of certain commodities, rather than as a noun. Indeed, these commodities considered money usually have certain qualities different from others: they are not usually consumable, they are divisible, scarce, transportable, easily sold—with a lot of liquidity—storable, fungible, they must facilitate quantification, be difficult to manipulate, be easy to

verify and not deteriorate with the passage of time. All these qualities are what allow these commodities to be used as a *means of exchange*, to be considered *good money*. In the end, money is a commodity whose main value is to facilitate exchanges, which is an essential function, since it reduces the costs of trading, which is why it is so fundamental in societies.

We can now see how Bitcoin fits in them:

- It is not consumable.

- Each bitcoin can be divided into 100 million *satoshis*.

- Bitcoin is scarce, since there will be 21 million at most, not counting those that are already lost.

- It is highly *liquid:*[iv] The Bitcoin market is global and operational 24/7.

[iv] There are three specializations in the functions of money, depending on supply:

• *Fiat* money can adjust supply to demand, which makes it maintain a certain price stability with a good monetary policy. However, its tendency is systematic devaluation, so it is a lousy reserve and deposit of value. It should, therefore, be considered a specialization in the function of unit of account and means of payment.

• Gold increases its supply in a similar way to what annual production does, 2% per year, so that, in average periods of time, it is an asset that reserves value well, allowing it to buy the same as in other periods. It is a specialization in the reserve of value.

• Bitcoin has a deterministic, limited supply, which, due to custody errors, will soon be deflationary. As the price of any commodity is fixed by supply and demand, volatility is something that will always remain with bitcoin, so it will be a bad medium to be unit of account, means of payment or store of value. However, it is the only real asset with a deflationary supply and a long-term growing demand for its properties, which makes it a specialization in the function of deposit of value to hoard balances that are not needed in the short and medium term. Therefore, Bitcoin is the best way to transfer value over time, understood as the long term.

Thus, we see how *fiat*, gold, and bitcoin are specializations in the functions of money, based on their ability to match supply to demand:

Fiat = short term = means of payment + unit of account = depreciation over time

Gold = reserve of value = stable over time

Bitcoin = deposit of value = appreciation in the long term

- It is easily storable, and its custody and storage costs are lower than those of any other asset with which it can compete.

- Money should be the fungible good par excellence, and what is more fungible than an identical digital asset?

- Bitcoin is easy to quantify, given its divisibility and global scale it allows the quantification of all goods and relationships at a global level.

- It is difficult to manipulate, its supply is immutable, and its issuance schedule is known in advance.

- Anyone can verify all transactions that have been made since the origin of Bitcoin.

- Bitcoin does not deteriorate over time, they do not age - advantages of cyberspace, and moreover, its transactions are immutable, irreversible.

Bitcoin fulfills all the desirable qualities of good money, on a new scale, with security and immutability never known before and redefining the right of ownership. Moreover, for all its characteristics of globality, security, impartiality, immutability, verifiability, and non-dependence on third parties, it would make it possible to reduce transaction costs in an increasingly international economy.

Bitcoin opens up a new world, a space of resistance and freedom.

Chapter 6

Redefining Property Rights

> If you have a great heritage, all you have to do is find one bank in Singapore that will treat you better than the bank in New York, or London, or Tokyo, and then you can move it in half an hour for five bucks. And what happens next? The bank in New York thinks, 'Well, I guess we can't screw these guys over because they will just move to Singapore' and the guys in California say, 'Well, I can't just tax all the Bitcoin in California, it will move to Wyoming, it will move to Singapore, it will move to Malta.' And at the end of the day, you could totally go fuck themselves, you can put it in your head, memorize the freaking key and it's here and then, you know, the classic Bitcoiner response is, "Oh, yeah, my bitcoin, I lost it in a boating accident." What it means is, at the end of the day, if you push me too far, I lost it, it's gone, sorry. TAX THAT!
>
> Michael Saylor on #Bitcoin

Bitcoin introduces many changes, although one of the most important is, undoubtedly, the fact that it redefines the concept of private property by making it dependent on knowledge, specifically on *keys*, a matter that seems counterintuitive, but is as simple as using a web page or a bank application.

That's right, Bitcoin redefines the right of private property by making it effective in such a way that it prevents confiscation. Once you have your keys—*not your keys, not your coins*—its technology allows you to stay out of reach of anyone, and in case you lose the device from which you usually access, you can regain access to your funds simply by knowing your *seed*—a set of words—that allow us to access to them on any other device.

The revolution is of such magnitude that it allows us to accumulate wealth without anyone else in the world being able to take it away from us, for better or for worse. It is a property contract without the need for States, it allows us to have exclusive control of a good without the need for laws or intermediaries. Moreover, it not only allows the accumulation of value but also allows it to be transmitted without depending on the State, from one end of the planet to the other, without anyone being able to prevent it. This, which seems difficult, has been the case for more than a decade. By eliminating dependence on a third party, you avoid the possibility of censorship or any limitation to your property and increase security by making property dependent on knowledge. This is a change never before known, or even considered, in history. Any corporeal good can be confiscated, but in cyberspace, the sovereignty of the State has no power, so new categories, that were simply unthinkable before because there was no such thing, can be built.

In today's societies, private property depends on the State: its regulation, its registers, its taxes and confiscations, its judicial decisions, its censorship. With Bitcoin, the global space is created in which they can neither take away what you have there, nor prevent you from sending it.

Chapter 7

Why Bitcoin Is Important, Not Blockchain

> It is sometimes said that a blockchain is immutable, and so Bitcoin is, just like any other. No, no, no, there is an important nuance.
>
> Emérito Quintana on #Bitcoin

It is often said that the important thing is not Bitcoin but *blockchain* technology. Well, this is one of the major errors on which a house of cards is being built, doomed to fall irredeemably. *Blockchain* has existed since 1991, however, no one had found any use for it until Bitcoin, since it only makes sense as it is used in it.

Why is the technology said to be more important than Bitcoin? Because Bitcoin is in a process of discovery by the market and its monetary qualities are not yet considered, so it is thought that the novelty has to be the technology it incorporates. Moreover, since it sounds like a decentralized, neutral, time-stamped record of information, it seems that it could be used for supply chains, for registering and transmitting bonds or shares, real estate ownership, etc.

These qualities are unique to the Bitcoin *blockchain*, including the system as a whole. Immutability is not a property of Bitcoin's code but is an emergent property of its incentive system. This is what makes Bitcoin irreplicable, since it is the consensus and incentive system what gives it security and integrity. As we have seen, Bitcoin solves the problem of double spending, for which an immutable record was needed, to avoid the possibility of sending the same digital monetary units twice and solve the problem of dependence on third parties too.

Well, as Polavieja points out:

> The first issue is that a computer system, blockchain-based or not, is incapable of autonomously verifying the existence and qualities of things that are external to the system itself. A computer registry of gold coins has no way of knowing whether a gold coin physically exists or not, whether it is authentic, where it is and who controls it. This information has to be provided by a third party.[5]

But there, you are already depending on someone else. If it were applied to trace the origin of this gold, it would not be possible to verify such a thing either, since this information would have to be entered by someone. For the computer system, it is only possible to verify products of their nature, in the case of Bitcoin it is a set of data internal to the system itself, so it avoids dependence on third parties for such verification.

The second problem is that even if the data is of the same nature as the system, to achieve immutability it is essential that anyone can easily and independently verify all the data from its source, but, I insist, without having to delegate to third parties. And therefore, it has to be difficult to manipulate, it is not enough to reveal that someone has manipulated the information.

This was solved by Satoshi through the brilliant idea of the *Proof of Work*. Let's see Emérito's explanation:

> In a *blockchain*, hash functions are used, which are a mathematical way of creating unique digital fingerprints of any information, fingerprints that are easy to verify. If any data changes, such as a block with transactions, the fingerprint (the hash) changes, evidencing the manipulation. To chain blocks, it is enough to include the hash of the previous block in the new one, so the new hash depends on the previous one. So, if we all have the same chain and someone changes something, we will notice. And so it is, but the important thing is not to realize that someone has made a modification (tamper-evident), that's not real security. The change does not have to be evident; it has to be practically impossible to modify anything (tamper-proof), that would make it secure and immutable. And that is not achieved by the blockchain.
>
> The Bitcoin network requires a proof of work for each block, it requires that the hash has a certain number of zeros, which can only be achieved by randomly testing. You can't pretend you've got a valid hash without incurring a significant energy cost. That is mining. The nodes in the network take as true the longest chain, the one with the most proof of work, the most evidence of accumulated energy [so any criticism of energy consumption is meaningless if you consider Bitcoin useful, as it is fundamental to guarantee its immutability]. In that scenario, even if you have 51% of the computational power, how do you change the past? how do you modify a transaction from 2 weeks ago? In Bitcoin that is an eternity, it is already engraved on stone under mountains of accumulated energy, a monument of immutability. A new category of immutability.
>
> And why do miners do it? For the reward, for the balanced system of economic incentives that protects the network, which

has gone through a process already irreplicable for others to try to imitate.

We just need a global Proof of Work system, there is no room for second best. The difference between tamper-evident and tamper-proof will be momentous as we review history.[6]

Therefore, any application employing *blockchain* that is not universally verifiable and immutable with data internal to the system itself and/or relies on third parties is all smoke and mirrors.

Chapter 8

Why Not Other Cryptocurrencies? What About the Environment!

Shrek: For your information, Bitcoin is more complex than people think.

Donkey: For example?

Shrek: For example? Bitcoin is like onions.

Donkey: Does it stink?

Shrek: No!

Donkey: Does it make you cry?

Shrek: Yes! No! Layers! Onions have layers! Bitcoin has layers! Onions have layers! Do you understand? They both have layers!

Donkey: Oh! They both have layers! But not everyone likes onions. DOGE! Everyone likes Doge! And they're made in layers!

Shrek: And why do I care... what people like! Bitcoin is not like shitcoins!

Donkey: And what do you think about Ethereum?

Shrek on #Bitcoin

Encompassing everything under the concept of cryptocurrency is probably the biggest mistake of all those related to the world of Bitcoin. It has been settled under this error and the previous one—*blockchain*—the idea that there are new, competing, disruptive alternatives, which raise an option to the established monetary system, and a race has begun to see which will be the next bitcoin. "There are thousands of cryptocurrencies, why is bitcoin going to be the winner? It's slow!"

The mistake, surely malicious, is to believe that the important thing about Bitcoin is that it is characterized by the use of cryptocurrency and certainly, Bitcoin uses it, but it is not what differentiates it from previous currencies. In fact, it was already in use long before Bitcoin. In this aspect, Bitcoin does not present a great novelty: It employs widely used standard algorithms. It does not bring any advances in cryptography, because it is not necessary.

And why don't all these currencies compete with bitcoin? Because they don't even try. As we have seen, one of its fundamental qualities is not to depend on third parties. If you already have a guaranteed system that has been working for more than a decade without depending on anyone, why would you want a cheap copy that can be manipulated at any time by an entity, a person, or a foundation? Rather than aiming for global monetary systems, they are business shares, at best, and neolatry systems at worst. If you think bitcoin is expensive, remember that you can always accumulate fractions of it: satoshis.

Not even a new technology would pose to be an alternative to Bitcoin, as that technology could be adopted because it is open source. Nor are there any monetary qualities of the ones we have seen, that outperform Bitcoin, which could also be adopted.

In short, none pose an alternative to Bitcoin, not even Ethereum, as it makes no sense to have large cash balances in a currency whose "virtue" is *smart contracts* and whose growth is based on the house of cards of *blockchain* technology and cryptocurrencies. We don't do *smart contracts* often, so small amounts of money will be used for these one-off contracts and demanding something to get rid of it immediately does not usually confer much value to an asset; although if speculation continues as to whether it will be the next bitcoin, it can always follow in its wake.

Hundreds of new *shitcoins* are sprouting up every day claiming to be the best because they are the fastest and least expensive, processing more transactions per second at a better price. But again, this is not understanding the problem that Bitcoin solves, we already had PayPal for that. What we are talking about is to allow universal verification without relying on third parties to avoid double-spending and for this, the slowness of the base layer is a virtue, not a defect, because it provides security. So that anyone can verify everything, Bitcoin limits the number of transactions that can be included in each block and maintains a certain time between blocks. This limitation is what makes the transaction cost of a shipment increase when demand exceeds this limited capacity. The cost is a consequence of demand since the capacity for a transaction to be included in the block is auctioned by first processing transactions from users who are willing to pay more, which is also part of the incentive system for securing bitcoin. We must remember that bitcoin is not for paying coffees, as neither is gold; we have no day-to-day problems for it, but for saving and having an asset as a store of value; although applications that allow cheap micropayments in other layers, such as *Lightning Network, can be implemented.*

At the origin of the internet, there was also a war, the protocol wars, where several types of communication protocols postulated as candidates to be the central system of decentralized communications and information at a global level, very similar to our current situation. Depending on what the market demands, Bitcoin will end up being imposed or not, in that war the TCP/IP protocol won because it allowed a higher degree of connectivity. In this war, Bitcoin is the most secure.

As for energy consumption, which is one of the most frequent criticisms, it is based on many errors. The main one is that Bitcoin is useless. Electric cars consume electricity too, but cars are useful and users pay for their electricity, that's it. Bitcoin is a global monetary system, 24/7, totally accessible, anyone can develop business on Bitcoin, it cannot be manipulated by politicians or bankers, etc. It seems useful and, therefore, reasonable that, to guarantee its immutability and security—as we have already seen—consumes the energy necessary to sustain the system. As if that were not enough, the possibility of the total delocalization of the energy consumption that the miners have to make could solve a large part of the energy waste that occurs in the world, since they will look for the cheapest energy and there is no cheaper energy than the one wasted from the production centers due to the costs of transferring it to the grid.

At the same time, it encourages forms of energy production that generate at a constant rate, such as hydroelectric power. Many renewable projects are discarded due to the volatility of their production with respect to the expected demand, which means that much of the time energy is wasted. Bitcoin solves these peaks by making these projects viable. And, as if that were not enough, it would make it possible to amortize electricity infrastructures in developing countries, which have a lot of overcapacity at the source.

But none of this compares to the real effect of mass adoption of Bitcoin by the majority of the population. Let me explain: Consumerism is what causes most of the environmental impact in our days. What would happen if a significant majority of the world had money that steadily revalues over time? They would tend to hoard it, to not consume so much by parting with it (it would lower their *time preference*). Bitcoin opens the possibility for everyone to save, to make more rational use of money:

> So, I believe that if we have a currency that is more deflationary, people will be incentivized, instead of going out and consuming really useless items, to save and invest in long-term projects. I'm a believer that it is not consumption that really drives long-term sustainable growth of the economy. What really increases our quality of life is long-term projects in technologies, research and things like that. The best things ever created were 10, 20, 30-year efforts, rather than going out and buying something useless, right?[7]
>
> *The Ultimate Bitcoin Argument*, Murad Mahmudov

Central Banks never cease to stimulate the economy by generating an ever-increasing money supply, which has the effect of creating new monetary units to spend, depreciating the currency itself. That is, today it is worth more than tomorrow and, therefore, that it is better to spend it and not hoard it, since if you leave it in the bank, it will lose value. The long-term impact of Bitcoin on the world could be to correct this consumerism, by having money worth hoarding instead of spending it on any object; and to prevent the credit expansion of central banks that generate hundreds of business projects doomed to fail and waste society's scarce resources.

Chapter 9

Volatility

> Volatility is information that has not yet been digested [...]
> There is no such thing as high volatility, what exists is incorrect
> exposure to a volatile asset.
>
> Adolfo Contreras on #Bitcoin

A mong the alleged criticisms of bitcoin, one of the most repeated is that it is very volatile, and indeed, it is. In fact, bitcoin is inherently volatile.[v] As its supply is limited and its issuance deterministic, the variation in price is mainly affected by changes in demand, which is never stable. But far from being a drawback, it is highly desirable. After all, without volatility, it would still be worth $1. Bitcoin is not a company, nor does it have a marketing department, it has to make itself known somehow.

New business projects are very difficult to evaluate. If you enter at the beginning, you run the risk of not succeeding. If you enter

---

[v] Nieto, F. (2022). "Why Is Bitcoin Inherently Volatile?"
https://gist.github.com/fernandonm/81cb21bdce0910055de32b98ee4119e1#file-inherent_volatility-pdf

at the end, you miss a unique business opportunity. Only with a proper investment thesis, where you analyze what you buy, you can properly value that asset and maintain the conviction in it regardless of its price. It's the same with soccer players: When stars are scarce and their price skyrockets, the transfer markets go crazy with the prices of future promises, trying to discern which one will be better and which one will be worse. This could serve as an analogy for Bitcoin if it were possible for any of them to compete, but "just as heaven cannot brook two suns, nor Earth, two masters."

It is such an ambitious asset that its value could far exceed the gold and silver market, but it is so novel that many believe that in the future it will be worth zero. If it becomes one of the most capitalized assets in the world in the future, it will be because the market will have discovered that it is a superior alternative to all of its competitors. As we will discuss in the next chapter, realizing this is the most asymmetric bet there is, but it is only beginning. Volatility, as Adolfo Contreras points out, is undigested information, an illuminated sign that people are realizing what is going on here that others can't even glimpse.

It was very expensive for me not to understand it at first, and if it hadn't been because it went up in price again—because it was still there when I thought it was dead—I wouldn't have paid attention to it. Volatility is what will enable its adoption, and the greater its adoption by understanding it, the less volatile it will be. Mass adoption of Bitcoin inevitably goes through volatility; because volatility is produced by people entering because they see others making money without understanding it, and fleeing when they see the price drop.

It is worth remembering here one of the mottos of the Bitcoin community: "HODL." Its origin lies in an anonymous publication from 2013, whose title was "I AM HODLING," due to the drunken state of its author. In it, he described that he was a terrible trader and could not predict the lows and highs like others, since the price of bitcoin was lower than when he acquired it. So, he concluded that traders could only take his money if he decided to sell. And that only a weak-minded person would sell based on fear. He was going to ignore his fear and keep his bitcoin—hopefully, our friend has HODL his bitcoin since then.

This story puts us before a reality: The difficulty of understanding Bitcoin derives in tremendous volatility, due to the asymmetry of information that exists in the market. The one who buys without knowing what he buys, does not know how much bitcoin is "worth," and when its price goes down, he will get scared and sell, or he will have a very bad time with volatility. That is why it is advisable to study it before. If you don't understand it and can't handle volatility, Bitcoin is not for you, at least for the time being. If you still want to be part of it: HODL!

Bitcoin doesn't have to do anything apart from what it has been doing for over a decade: immune to all the noise around it and going at its own pace. It will do just that: "When he woke up, Bitcoin was still there."

Chapter 10

Bitcoin Versus Its Alternatives

We choose volatile growth over stable debasement.

Vijay Boyapati on #Bitcoin

I t is convenient to define the field because it competes against everything to which its users stop allocating their current currency. But by the nature of the good, Bitcoin is an asset among another class of assets, those that act as a medium of exchange, which can be either between other people—transfer of ownership—or exchanges with my "future self"—ownership over time. Today's *fiat* currencies meet these requirements, but they are not the only ones. Bonds, shares, deposits, gold, real estate, government debt, investment, pension funds, art, etc., are also characterized by this, as they act in a significant percentage as a store of value.

These assets, as we can see, can be both tangible and intangible—contracts—and in order to keep a good record of their ownership, they depend to a great extent on the States, both in terms of their regulation, contracts, and property, as well as their needs, monetary expansion, and taxes. Therefore, their security depends on the State, something that could cause problems if the State were to enter into *crisis*. Moreover, since the invention of the telegraph, tangible goods have been inefficient as a record of property, and abstractions such as vouchers, contracts, or digitizations have been made to streamline and reduce the costs of trading them. Likewise, the supply of all these assets varies from the currencies of the States, which can create as much as they want, to gold, whose supply increases between 1.6% and 2% per year.

Likewise, within these assets some have counterparty risk, that is, one of the parties fails to comply with its obligation. For example, having a cash deposit when the entity goes bankrupt and not being able to withdraw your money. Others have redenomination risk, that is to say, the proportional substitution of one currency for another. For example, zeros have been removed from the currency on several occasions in Venezuela. Or, in a hypothetical case of a breakup of the euro, the countries that remain outside will have to return to their devalued national currencies.

However, in return for these assets, the State provides some security (depending on the country in question), although a brief history of the economy quickly shows that the general trend is to devalue currencies, raise taxes, provide slow justice, and impose heavy regulations and confiscations. And yes, even gold has been confiscated.

> There is nothing better for men to orient their economic interests correctly than to observe the great benefits obtained by those more skillful individuals who decided to accept, for a long time, goods of high saleability in exchange for all the others.
>
> Carl Menger on #Bitcoin

Facing all these assets, what role does bitcoin play? We have already seen many of its properties:

- It is an excellent register of property, immutable and public.
- Anyone can verify transactions.
- It does not depend on third parties.
- Bitcoin redefines the right of ownership and makes it difficult to confiscate in practice.
- It is not within the reach of regulations, expropriations, or taxes.
- Its supply is limited to 21 million, so there is no dilution of your share of the pie.
- Being a real asset, it has no counterparty risk.
- The limitation of its supply prevents the risk of redenomination.

In return, it has a strong component of individual responsibility, as you become the custodian of your funds, and that implies certain diligence, but even when it comes to that, it presents novelties, as it opens up a new range of ways to manage and take responsibility for your assets, including through functionalities that are continually being developed, such as *TimeLock* or multi-signature portfolios.

Honestly, I do not think that Bitcoin will compete in the short- and medium-term to be a means of everyday payment—no matter how much progress the *Lightning Network* makes. That is not a problem in most countries, so it will not be in great demand as a solution. In fact, PayPal already existed when Bitcoin appeared, and conventional *fiat* currencies are enough, at least for the time being. Undoubtedly, it is a great competitor with those currencies that show strong devaluations, with long-term deposits, with those shares that are used as a store of value (those of more consolidated companies with defensive moats) and undoubtedly with gold, public debt, real estate, and art. Whether it will compete with the dollar or the euro in the long term remains to be seen.

Expansionary monetary policies around the world have done nothing but devalue currencies. Flooding the money market has meant that most citizens had to become part-time investors, investing their savings in the type of assets we have been discussing, since leaving the earnings from their work in the bank meant constantly losing value. This has led to an over-dimensioning of the fixed income and equity markets, as well as in *real estate* since the purchase of real estate has been consolidated as a safe value, hence the exorbitant prices we see in the main cities of the world.

Likewise, the decline of the welfare States, together with demographics, does not bode well for these States' ability to sustain their political promises to pay pensions and other social benefits. And this results in another problem: They will need to collect higher taxes, so they will raise taxes on these assets, especially on the most illiquid ones such as real estate and pension funds. And it's better not to talk about the risk of a bubble in public debt or art.

This growing nervousness has brought to the market a growing and more complex number of financial products and services, which implies a high risk of information asymmetry between the parties, and always with the regulatory risk present. Let's see why Bitcoin is better than these assets in many ways.

Bitcoin's main advantages over all its competitors are its nature, custody and preservation costs, its shipping and liquidity costs, and its risks with respect to its alternatives. Its main disadvantages are custody risks, which imply certain liability and its volatility, although we have already discussed the latter, as well as its nature.

Regarding its custody and conservation costs: Bitcoin is very cheap to keep since only one wallet is needed—there are many types—and if you do not want to do it yourself you can always assign custody to a third party, although this reduces one of its virtues: the lack of dependence on third parties. There are no conservation costs since, in cyberspace, they do not age. Moreover, it is a field in which progress is constantly being made with security measures such as multi-signature, *TimeLock*, *passphrase*, to mention a few. What is the cost of guarding gold? What is the cost of conservation and surveillance of a building or a work of art?

Shipping costs and liquidity: In Bitcoin, shipping costs vary depending on network saturation. They do not usually represent a significant amount and allow sending as much value as a dollar or millions of them, relatively fast and cheap; while its liquidity is very high, with a global market that works 24/7 without anyone being able to stop it or prevent it. How much does it cost to send hundreds of millions in gold? And in works of art? How to liquidate a billion in real estate assets?

There are four types of risk: regulatory, counterparty, supply, and conflict risks.

Regulatory risks: Money in circulation, regulations and taxes have experienced remarkable growth in recent decades, and nothing seems to indicate that the trend will change. Bitcoin, on the other hand, offers a space of freedom and security, and therefore, peace of mind, where you are not affected. What are the chances that States will stop devaluing their currencies? What are the prospects that regulations will not increase? What can we expect from taxes on all assets, especially the most illiquid ones, after a crisis like Coronavirus? Will politicians leave private pension funds intact knowing that there is money accumulated there?

Counterparty risks: There have been many times a third party has breached its obligation. All development of law throughout history is due, precisely, to the fact that some breach their obligations and contracts. Bitcoin is a real asset, a present good you have—that is why it does not have to be backed by anything—it has no risk of someone not giving it to you unless you keep it in an exchange or under the custody of a third party—*not your keys, not your bitcoin*. Has a bank ever failed and not been able to return the money to its depositors? Has a State ever failed and not been able to meet its obligations? Has a company ever failed and not been able to meet its obligations? Too many.

Supply risks: Bitcoin's supply is fixed; there are 21 million units and we know its issuance schedule in advance. How many dollars can be issued? Let's not even talk about other currencies:

Who can guarantee that a competitor of the company you own shares in will not appear and drive it out? Will it be possible to continue issuing public debt at these levels indefinitely?

Risks due to conflicts: Bitcoin is impossible to confiscate and does not depend on third parties, so its portability is total and its invulnerability is very high. You can cross a border with millions of dollars in your head. Most of the world lives in safe places, but what guarantee is there that it will stay that way forever? History is nothing but the succession of conflicts between different powers, "War never changes."[vi] In case it happens, how much of your wealth would be safe or could you take with you and liquidate it anywhere in the world?

We are still in the early days of Bitcoin, in a process of discovery of its qualities by the market; it seems to me that its advantages over its competitors are many.

[vi] Famous quote from the Fallout video game saga.

Part 3

States and Central Banks Versus Bitcoin

Chapter 11

About the State

The State is not a general concept applicable to all peoples and times. Rather, it is a specific historical concept linked to a particular period; the second half of the sixteenth century, in which its first beginnings are situated, certainly decisive, and only comes to fruition one or two centuries later [...] From the civil wars of religion arises in France the idea of the sovereign political decision that neutralizes all theological-ecclesial antagonisms [...] In this situation the concepts of state and sovereignty found in France its first and decisive legal embodiment. With this, the organizational form of the Sovereign State became part of the conscience of the peoples of Europe, making the State, according to the vision of the following centuries, the only normal form in which political unity is manifested par excellence.

Carl Schmitt against #Bitcoin

A s I commented in the prologue, the purpose of this book is to provoke a crisis about two beliefs. The first, that a currency that is money must have the backing of political authority. I believe I have succeeded in making a reasoned case for why this assertion is not only unnecessary, but why Bitcoin is that "cunning introduction" of which Hayek spoke about, and the reasons why it is the best candidate for it. Provoking an earthquake in the second belief, that "State" is a concept that can be applied to any political society and that post-State political forms are not to be thought of, will be the object of these chapters. Carl Schmitt is probably the greatest political thinker of the twentieth century. In his *Theory of the Constitution*, Schmitt deals specifically with this question, along with an article in which he develops it: *The State as a concrete concept linked to a historical epoch.*

The misunderstanding—to call any political form a State—has its origin in the development of Political Science in the nineteenth century in Germany where, when studying the Greek Polis as a paradigm of the political, they translated it as the city-state—*StadtStaat*—which in German are almost homophones, so that the categories of the wrongly called modern state—there is no other State than the modern one—were applied to the Greek *Polis*, which ended up extending to all political realities. The diffusion of Hegel and Marx's thought ended up extending this error to other great thinkers who came later, and it was also reflected in the translations of previous thinkers, even attributing the term *State* to Spinoza, who used *Imperium*; and even to Aristotle who used the term *koinonia*—political community. Thus, as there was a void, a gap, for a word designating the political—the unity of each political reality—the term *State* filled that space—hence for our time every possible political form is State and the debate revolves mainly around whether it is necessary to increase or reduce the size of the State, but no new political forms are proposed.

This has resulted in considering the State eternal, either by equating it with institutionalized coercion, or by considering that before it, there were tribes, but that before the State, there were no politics and, consequently, that there is nothing that can happen to it. The State is nothing more than a political form of a concrete epoch, as Schmitt's quotation well reminds us, and for this reason, it is transitory, a *historical idea*. What always governs is the Government, not the State, since it is always a minority that governs, as Robert Michels pointed out.[vii] For this reason, the history of political philosophy is about good government, and not about the good historical-political form, which has been diverse over time: the *Polis*, the *Roman Urbs*, the *Civitas* or *Res Publica Christiana*, the Byzantine Basilea, or the State itself.

This reality can be appreciated through the distinction between *auctoritas* and *potestas*. *Auctoritas*—authority—is the socially recognized knowledge, to which certain functions are attributed because of its knowledge of the matter. *Potestas* is the power entrusted with maintaining the concrete order of a political community. For example, classic law in Rome was a matter of authority, or in this case, of jurisprudents—those who specialized in determining what was fair in a specific case—and there was no legal norm emanating from the political power that determined what they had to judge as fair. For this reason, there was a sharp separation between the two powers. Bodin, through the idea of *sovereignty*, merges both concepts into one, in such a way that the sovereign will be both authority and power. Let us think of the image of Hobbes' *Leviathan* clutching a sword and a crosier, symbols of traditional power and authority.

[vii] As for the number of those who govern, it does not matter whether it is a dictatorship or a dictatorship or a democracy, they cannot govern all or only one; it is always an oligarchy that steers the course.

The State, as a historical reality, has its origin in the process of the Catholic Church rupturing as a result of Protestantism, together with the territorial consequences of the discovery of America by the Spanish Empire. As the globe is completed, the *lymes*—formerly there were no delimited borders but gray spaces—gave way to closed borders, and the universalism of the Spanish Catholic Empire project is on the wane, giving way to particularism, both religious and political, taking shape after the Peace of Westphalia in 1648. It was in the treaty of that peace, where the principle of territorial integrity was established, and on it would be erected a power whose characteristic would be sovereignty. These monarchies, which became absolute, would give rise to an apparatus of power that would become independent of them, the State, which took possession of the sovereignty—an attribute only corresponding to God—allowing the one who obtains the government to be the usufructuary of it. It is no coincidence that it arises from the wars of religion:

> The modern state develops by the prince becoming 'absolute.' [...] The political formations originating in this way were absolute monarchies. The 'absolute' character lies in the fact that the prince is *'legibus solutus.'* For political reasons, on which he alone decides, the prince has the authority and capacity to disregard the legitimate demands of the estates and the existing privileges and agreements. [...] This modern state is sovereign; its state authority is indivisible.[8]
>
> *Constitutional Theory*, Schmitt

Bodin defined Sovereignty in his *Six Books of the Commonwealth* as follows:

> Just as, according to the canonists, the Pope can never tie his own hands, so the sovereign prince cannot bind himself, even if he wishes. For this reason, edicts and

ordinances conclude with the formula 'FOR SUCH IS
OUR GOOD PLEASURE', thus intimating that the laws
of a sovereign prince, even when founded on truth and
right reason, proceed simply from his own free will.[9]

Political power has always had religious connotations, but Bodin
attributes directly to the monarch a divine, *sacred* quality. This
concept produces the radical split of the monarchy—which now
holds the sovereignty—from its political community, since
previously power did not determine the law, but it was to some
extent subject to it and remained on the margins of it. There was
a clear distinction between authority and power since the
authority—socially recognized knowledge—was the Catholic
Church and its jurists, and the power were the monarchs.[viii] By
abandoning the universal Church to form its particular
projects—its States—the power absorbed the authority,
remaining above the Church and the Law, and making the Law.
In this way, the absolute monarch remained as a demiurge for
society, in which he was in charge of organizing and creating
order at his will.

As for Hobbes, the great theologian of the State, the sovereignty
that Bodin attributes to the monarch, making it absolute, Hobbes
transfers it to the apparatus of government power—the State—
creating the Leviathan, that *Deus mortalis*. If something is
inherent to the State, it is sovereignty, whose main value as an
authority is security: "Without the State, there is no freedom,
freedom is the fruit of the security that I provide," could be its
leitmotif. He characterizes the state of nature as a state of

---

[viii] Dalmacio Negro explains it as follows: "The prince, sovereign as usufructuary in his
own right of the sovereignty owned by the State, is the source of Law. Bodin united the
natural supremacy of the political, the supremacy over the juridical, the right to make
laws to create new situations. Until then it was necessary to discover in each case the
meaning of the Law, a mission entrusted to the judges." Negro, D. (2010). Historia de las
formas del Estado. Una introducción, El buey mudo, pp. 134–135.

constant war, where everyone can suffer violence from everyone else, every man would have to live in fear of his neighbor; although these ideas probably have more to do with Hobbes' personality, who recognizes in his autobiography, "*My mother gave birth to twins: myself and fear.*"[ix]

When Bodin developed the concept of sovereignty, he included the right to coin money as one of its fundamental components. Governments realized that this monopolized right was very lucrative and granted great power. An attack on this function would be a direct attack on sovereignty, and therefore, on the State. Let us keep in mind once again what I commented when speaking of the *Philosophy of Money*, that it had a desacralizing character.

> Anyone who recognizes the state will no longer hold that the state's power is original or absolute; rather, this is the dogma of a believer. In the believer's realm of experience, the existence of man loses its reality. Instead, the state takes over the reality and makes itself into the only true reality, from which a stream of reality is allowed to flow back to the people, providing them with new stimulus in their role as parts of the superhuman reality. We are caught in the innermost heart of a religious experience, and our words describe a mystical process.[10]

> *The Political Religions*, Eric Voegelin

If money had a secularizing character and a *destructive* character, it is inherent to any new technology—its destruction being proportional to the innovation it represents. I believe that with these considerations we can already glimpse part of the origin of

---

[ix] His mother gave birth to him early due to the fear she suffered from the arrival of the Invincible Armada.

the crisis facing the States: If their essence, sovereignty, loses one of its mainstays—the exclusive right to mint money—for a technological and conceptual innovation which, being monetary, desacralizes it, it will not take long for them to lose their religious aura; and if it is revealed as a *historical idea* incapable of fulfilling its function, they will collapse. But not before putting up a fight, and not only against Bitcoin, but also between different States.

Chapter 12

Crisis of the State

> Above this race of men stands an immense and tutelary power, which takes upon itself alone to secure their gratifications, and to watch over their fate. That power is absolute, minute, regular, provident, and mild. It would be like the authority of a parent, if, like that authority, its object was to prepare men for manhood; but it seeks on the contrary to keep them in perpetual childhood: it is well content that the people should rejoice, provided they think of nothing but rejoicing. For their happiness such a government willingly labors, but it chooses to be the sole agent and the only arbiter of that happiness: it provides for their security, foresees, and supplies their necessities, facilitates their pleasures, manages their principal concerns, directs their industry, regulates the descent of property, and subdivides their inheritances—what remains, but to spare them all the care of thinking and all the trouble of living?
>
> *Democracy in America*, Tocqueville on #Bitcoin

There is a global atmosphere of uncertainty, where anxiety is becoming generalized, unconsciously assimilating things will not go back to the way they were before. A few years ago, if you did not feel comfortable in the environment of your country, you could go to another one. But now the question is, "Which one if they are all the same?" It has been installed in the collective subconscious that young people will live worse than their parents, which is not surprising since the previous generation has already grown up and has barely been able to form a life project. Two generations know nothing but crisis, the one in 2008 and now the one of COVID-19.

When they consider the mere idea of a life project, they cannot help thinking that they have it tough. It is not something that depends on whether they work hard or not; it is a generalized historical circumstance. Discouragement is followed by the renunciation of aspirations to settle for a *standard* life hopefully.

One of the great changes we have not yet assimilated, and to which we have not paid as much attention as we should, is the increase in life expectancy. It is one of the greatest advances we have made, and I do not doubt that it will continue to increase during this century, at least for a significant part of the population. However, our societies were not designed to undergo this great change in such a short period, and the slowness of governments to introduce changes, in addition to the few incentives they have to carry them out, has further aggravated the situation. I am not only talking about welfare state systems, which did not foresee paying pensions for such long periods, but also referring specifically to the crisis of the institution of inheritance, as inheritance made it possible for children to start their life projects in their youth. The significant increase in life expectancy means that this capital that allows the start of such projects has not yet been transferred. It is now inherited, in most cases, in the twilight of life, when we become seniors. This concentrates on those who are over 65 years old; most of the purchasing power, since they not only have pensions but also inherit and are real estate owners which they rent to young people at astronomical prices. Hence the precariousness of young people, who cannot start their life projects and depend on their ascendants, is the norm and not the exception, not to mention the fact that these generations have gone into debt on their behalf for decades to come.

The fact that young people have no future prospects is a danger for our societies, and it is not the first time this has happened:

> State intervention; the absorption of all spontaneous social effort by the State, that is to say, of spontaneous historical action, which in the long-run sustains, nourishes, and impels human destinies. When the mass suffers any ill-fortune or simply feels some strong appetite, its great temptation is that permanent, sure possibility of obtaining everything without effort, struggle, doubt, or risk merely by touching a button and setting the mighty machine in motion. The mass says to itself, 'L'Etat, c'est moi,' which is a complete mistake. [...] The result of this tendency will be fatal. Spontaneous social action will be broken up over and over again by State intervention; no new seed will be able to fructify. Society will have to live for the State, man for the governmental machine. And as, after all, it is only a machine whose existence and maintenance depend on the vital supports around it, the State, after sucking out the very marrow of society, will be left bloodless, a skeleton, dead with that rusty death of machinery, more gruesome than the death of a living organism. [...] The latter begins to be enslaved, to be unable to live except in the service of the State. The whole of life is bureaucratised. What results? The bureaucratisation of life brings about its absolute decay in all orders. Wealth diminishes, births are few.[11]

> *The Revolt of the Masses*, Ortega y Gasset

Now we do have a space in which we can escape from the State, be able to guard our income to be able to plan for the future and avoid the State sucking our marrow. And it is no small thing in our extremely polarized societies to have such a refuge.

There is also a clear divergence between the interests of many wealthy people and the state. Historically, great fortunes have been made hand in hand with politics, and in our time, it is no different, but with phenomena such as globalization and the decentralization of new technologies. Many millionaires have made their fortunes outside politics. If an economic and political crisis occurs, what fortune will be safe from the State's voracious tax collection? The circumstance we are facing is to some extent new because now they will be able to avoid it, which will surely lead to the so-called "secession of the rich." Who, in turn, will tend to look for safer regions to settle in, as well as ways to save their wealth, and no doubt they will do so against a wounded State, we shall see if mortally wounded.

If this happens, and nothing leads me to think otherwise, we will have to look for new political forms, since this means the end of the possibility of redistribution by the State, a quality that has arrogated to itself as a justifying reason for its existence, that of being the provider of social reality. And it is especially important to open the field of political imagination since the end of the State is not the end of politics. Greed and the expansion of State competencies can result in losing everything, and in case it cannot fulfill the expectations it has generated, it can lead a significant part of the population—especially among the young—to a crisis in the belief in political power and a fall into anarchy. This thinking is fueled by the negative perception of the power of liberalism, leading to individualism. I think this is a mistake because men are *political animals*, as Aristotle said, and it is not convenient to go against the nature of things. If the State falls, we will have to build new political forms and not abandon ourselves to anarchy, as the government is indeed eternal, and men need to be guided towards virtue.

Looking at Bitcoin and its possible consequences, it could be suggested that its usefulness is only individual if it is able to remain outside the State and have a space of freedom, and indeed this is its primary usefulness. But this utility immediately becomes collective when the political power that has overreached its functions has to correct its direction by recovering its principles. Hence something new that restricts its possibilities need not be negative, given that its present tendency threatens to put an end to many historical societies. Returning to the government of men and abandoning the mechanism of the State may be its greatest utility since it will only be able to do what the citizens allow it to. The importance of Bitcoin's success may also have a positive function for politics.

The fact is that States, far from being a barrier to so-called *globalism*, are the gateway to it. If Globalism puts historical homelands at risk, it is not because of the opposition of States, but because of their express collaboration. Therefore Bitcoin, between globalism and patriotism, opens another way to explore other political forms. Despite aspiring to be a global currency, it does not go with the former, because it does not depend on third parties; and because it affects States to a great extent, it does not go against the latter either, because it will force governments to channel themselves.

In short, the feeling of generalized uncertainty is not unjustified, it is precisely in times of crisis that great men arise to make decisions, and it is in our hands building and thinking about new political forms.

Chapter 13

What Can States Do Against Bitcoin?

> Bitcoin changes everything...for the better. And we will forever work to make bitcoin better. No person (or institution) can change it or stop it.
>
> Jack Dorsey on #Bitcoin

othing.

Chapter 14

What Can States Do Against Bitcoin's Community and Adoption?

> At first, they say it's "theoretically impossible."
>
> Then, "Maybe it's possible, but it's certainly not practical."
>
> Then, "But only fringe groups are using it."
>
> Later, "We're studying it."
>
> Now, "It's the future. We are here to provide governance and regulation."
>
> Timothy May on #Bitcoin

The previous chapter may seem pretentious. How can States do nothing against Bitcoin, if Elon Musk says something against it and its price plummets? Certainly, we have already seen that the volatility in its price is very high because of the asymmetry of information. Since the vast majority does not understand its nature given that it is in a process of discovery, and the States can make its price go up and down without difficulty. Every few months, there is news that China has "banned" it, but how can they ban something that does not depend on third parties? What they usually ban is the conversion to their national currency in exchanges; but they can't do anything against Bitcoin, and it has been this way for more than a decade. They can attack Bitcoiners, miners, exchanges, but what can they expect to achieve against a digital, global, knowledge-dependent asset with a 24/7 market?

They can slow down their adoption, no doubt about it. Bad press, distraction with their digital currencies, CBDCs (Central Bank Digital Currency), using the term "cryptocurrencies," raising taxes, etc., are measures that will undoubtedly delay its adoption. But if Bitcoin is still there over the years while everything else fails, have they not done to it the greatest possible favor by singling it out as an enemy?

Another question to keep in mind is what happens in the event that it is adopted by a country's companies in a significant way, will the State go against the interests of its own companies?

What Can States Do for Bitcoin?

> Ask not what Bitcoin can do for you, ask what your
> country can do for Bitcoin.
>
> John F. Kennedy on #Bitcoin

History is nothing more than the stark struggle between the different political powers to impose themselves. If a qualitatively superior and scarce asset appears, the incentive to adopt it in a significant way should be very high. The competitive advantages it can offer in terms of both financing and increased purchasing power are considerable. Moreover, its success may particularly affect some countries, so why not use it as a weapon?

In my opinion, the most intelligent strategy they can follow is its adoption by the States themselves, their companies, and their citizens; it will give the first ones a lot of power over the last ones who enter; it will allow them to pay their huge debts and maintain their spending policies. Its adoption and the incentive to its adoption by their companies and citizens, as well as teaching them what it consists of, will give them a lot of advantage over the rest. Being a *Bitcoin-friendly* country can also be especially interesting if you want to attract all the capital that is looking for a safe place to settle. Not to mention all the jobs that will be created around it and the possibilities that it opens up and are yet to be explored, such as, for example, working from home and getting paid in bitcoin from anywhere in the world. Attracting human capital and large assets has never seemed so easy.

States are at odds with each other; they do not constitute a homogeneous and harmonious whole, so I consider it inevitable that such scenarios will occur, where different policies are adopted with respect to Bitcoin, although undoubtedly many will cling to their currencies, even if they die with them:

> I think it's a combination of incompetence and outright grasping for power. And I do believe that this will eventually happen to all *fiat* currencies around the world, but it will happen stage by stage. Of course, the second and third world currencies will be the first to collapse, and the more established euros, then the dollar. The financial leak from there towards Bitcoin will be a bit more gradual. It will be more like an "S" curve, and then it will reach a point where money will flow rapidly into Bitcoin because as I've described, people will simply realize that this money is harder than the other money. The other money, there are people behind it and these people can do whatever they want. However, this is governed by such a strong unbreakable algorithm and the community of people strengthens it in such a way, that I think the credibility, faith, and trust in Bitcoin relative to *fiat* currencies will keep growing. And as I said at the beginning, currencies, and sort of the cognitive monetary premium that is placed on them is first and foremost a matter of trust and credibility.[12]

> *The Definitive Bitcoin Argument*, Murad Mahmudov

Bitcoin and the States

> Past is not a hand-to-hand fight. The future overcomes it
> by swallowing it.
>
> *The Revolt of the Masses*, Ortega y Gasset on #Bitcoin

Bitcoin is a torpedo to the State's waterline. States have three ways of financing their expenditures: (1) through taxes, (2) through public debt, and (3) through inflation (inflation as an increase in the money supply, the increase in prices is a consequence that can follow from this). Bitcoin attacks all three lines.

First, it prevents the control of what is held in Bitcoin, as it is not confiscated. Therefore, it implies a series of very considerable limits and new challenges for the States, for which they are not prepared.

Secondly, it is an asset that, as we have seen, will compete directly with public debt, which means that governments—in debt—will be forced to raise interest rates in order to attract investment to their public debt in the face of bitcoin. This could lead them to financial tensions that end up bursting the public debt bubble and causing them serious difficulties in meeting their expenses.

Third, if they do not want a massive and rapid adoption of bitcoin, the best thing they can do is to offer a currency that does not depreciate steadily, so their best asset is to keep their currencies stable. The moment they depreciate or make exorbitant monetary expansions, they will have more than considerable problems with the flight to other options, among which bitcoin has every chance of becoming hegemonic. In addition, being forced to make spending containment policies, and even cutbacks, may entail a very high political cost, and if they have limitations to their monetary policy, they will have serious difficulties to maintain their deficits and high spending.

As if that were not enough, if bitcoin, as a qualitatively superior store of value, displaces a significant part of the value deposited in real estate, gold, and public debt, it will directly affect the solvency of States and banks. It should not be forgotten that the currency they currently issue is a liability of the central bank, which, in order to maintain its value, backs its assets with public debt, loans to banks for mortgages, loans to companies, and gold. If these assets are depreciated rapidly due to the appearance of a competitor superior to them in many respects, their solvency will follow suit, depreciating the currencies they issue and generating considerable "inflation," an effect similar to what would occur in the event of a cancellation of the public debt held by the States.

Yes, *fiat* money is a liability of the central bank, this is much clearer if we remember that until not so long ago it was convertible into gold. You could exchange banknotes for their equivalent in gold, the bank was required to have both gold as an asset and gold-convertible banknotes as a liability, at least in the proportion established by the law. Once Nixon ended the gold standard, money continued to be a liability. But if it was not convertible, what was their obligation? It was to maintain its purchasing power, to control its price and, as the price is regulated by supply and demand, central banks had to have mainly public debt in their assets, in order to be able to offer it in the market in case they have to influence its price by withdrawing *fiat* money from it.

But if, as I said, this had less demand because a more attractive competing asset appears, they will not be able to absorb all the *fiat* money they want from the market, so they may find it difficult to maintain control over their monetary policies. And if their money loses credibility because they cannot control it, it will also lose demand, producing a flight to other assets. Perhaps it would be advisable for them to start hoarding bitcoin as well.

All this implies is drastically limiting its capacity to distribute wealth and public spending, so that the masses who have placed their lives and their trust in the State may fear a great decrease in their life expectancy. If this happens, the crisis of the State will be total, since its essence is Sovereignty, the power that guarantees security and the knowledge—the authority—that gives it the aura to use the former; its discredit would imply its end. That's why, as I said at the beginning, Bitcoin is the greatest weapon against the State.

> Nations are wading deeper and deeper into an ocean of boundless debt. Public debts, which at first were a security to governments by interesting many in the public tranquility, are likely in their excess to become the means of their subversion. If governments provide for these debts by heavy impositions, they perish by becoming odious to the people. If they do not provide for them, they will be undone by the efforts of the most dangerous of all parties—I mean an extensive, discontented monied interest, injured and not destroyed.[13]
>
> *Reflections on the Revolution in France*, Edmund Burke

Chapter 15

Central Banks and Economic Crises: A Dead-End Street

> The main result at this stage is that the chief blemish of the market order which has been the cause of well-justified reproaches, its susceptibility to recurrent periods of depression and unemployment, is a consequence of the age-old government monopoly of the issue of money.
>
> *The Denationalization of Money*. Yes, Hayek again on #Bitcoin

Central banks, whose main mission is to carry out monetary policy, are an integral part of the current financial system and governments. If they become incapable of controlling their monetary policy or enter into crisis, they can directly drag down the States, since they are their main indirect financiers.

A very significant part of the recurrent crises of capitalism has their origin in monetary causes, in the policies carried out precisely by the central banks. The most widespread practice among them is to carry out an expansive monetary policy, that is, to significantly increase the monetary mass, which reaches society through loans to companies and the financing of the States and their public spending. It is a way of stimulating the economy, similar to the way one drinks coffee to wake up in the morning. However, when you can't live without coffee, and you need to drink more and more to have the same stimulating effect, then you have a problem. This situation is very similar to the one in which our economies are "stimulated" by *quantitative easing* (QE) policies.

The artificially cheap credit granted through these liquidity injections encourages the entrepreneur to initiate business projects that they would not carry out under other financing conditions and the States to increase their public spending. However, this has effects on the entire productive structure, producing a distortion in prices that leads entrepreneurs to be unable to adequately complete the projects they had started precisely with the easy money offered by these policies. When this is discovered by the market, the so-called crises are produced, which generate unemployment, waste of resources and efforts of society, frustration in those entrepreneurs who have not been able to complete their projects and a painful readjustment in societies.

This is due to this artificial expansion of credit without a correlative increase in previous savings, the cause of a series of effects—which I will explain below—that we call *economic cycles*.[14] Its explanation is probably the greatest contribution of the Austrian School of Economics.[x]

The first effect produced is that of important growth in the price of the factors of production demanded by the entrepreneur for

---

[x] The best explanation I have found in this respect is found in Huerta de Soto's Dinero, crédito bancario y Ciclos económicos, chapters V and VI. I will try to follow him and, if necessary, to paraphrase him shamelessly, although I will not hold him responsible for the interpretative bias, whose possible errors will be mine alone.

the new monetary units they have received from the banks in the process of credit expansion. Since there has been no growth in savings, resources have not been released—they have not stopped being consumed—from the stages closer to consumption, and the only way to attract them to these investment projects is to pay an additional premium for them. The same goes for the rest of the factors of production.

Releasing resources is a euphemistic way of putting it, but let's look at it with an example. If a group of citizens save money by no longer going to restaurants for dinner, those restaurant workers become unemployed, but they can be hired by employers for those longer-term projects that are precisely those that the citizens will buy with the money they are saving. If these citizens do not save in a way that frees up resources in the present and can finance such projects, but money is created out of thin air to finance them, employers will have to pay an additional premium, such as offer that worker something more than the salary they are currently earning, to incorporate them into their project. Since economic agents have not saved, they will not have money available in the future to buy the goods they start to produce. This creates an imbalance between what entrepreneurs produce and what citizens will demand in the future. The discovery of this imbalance is what triggers crises.

So, the first effect that can be observed is an increase in the price of labor, wages, raw materials, capital goods, and natural resources demanded by entrepreneurs. This increase is a first wake-up call because when they made their projects and their budgets, they considered certain prices for certain factors of production that are now being increased. This means they are already beginning to see that they are not going to obtain the benefits they expected.

The second effect that can be observed is the growth in the price of consumer goods and services as money spreads gradually and in stages throughout society. Money from the monetary expansion, which is first given to the States and companies, gradually spreads throughout society. As consumers now have more monetary units, they devote themselves to consume goods and services of immediate consumption, when the effect of increasing the production of consumer goods and services has not yet taken place, because the entrepreneurial projects which have been started have not yet matured.

The third effect is that of disparity in the profits of companies operating along with the productive structure of society. As the prices of consumer goods grow at a faster rate, the profits of companies operating in the sectors closer to consumption, in accounting and relative terms, are better than the profits of capital goods companies that have not yet been able to complete their investment projects and are seeing how their productive factors are costing more and more.

The fourth is the effect on interest rates. When monetary units are created out of thin air and injected into the system by lending them to entrepreneurs, the conditions demanded in exchange for the loans and the interest rate are reduced so that they are encouraged to borrow more. But when these additional monetary units have already been lent, the prices of consumer goods start to grow and "inflation" begins to occur; interest rates return to their previous level, and even in nominal terms to a higher level, because they foresee the loss of purchasing power of the monetary unit. And that causes the present value of capital goods to fall.

The fifth is the Cantillon effect. If the prices of consumer goods grow at a fast pace, faster than wages, it means that real wages tend to fall. This is a signal to entrepreneurs that they should use more labor and less capital goods, which were just the investment projects that had been undertaken by them in the bubble stage. As a result, capital goods remain unsold and bankruptcies, suspensions of payments, layoffs, and a defaulting increase begin. Entrepreneurs, "deceived" by the easy credit they have received from the banks, have undertaken overly ambitious investment projects that are not sustainable and are only profitable in the circumstances of the bubble when interest rates were so low.

Economic crises bring to light the fact that these investment projects produce capital goods that are not in demand, thus squandering society's scarce resources and diverting the energies of workers and entrepreneurs to projects doomed to fail. Because of these policies, the productive structures of the society affected by them tend to shorten and focus on the sectors closest to consumption, leaving aside those business projects that require a longer period for their maturation.

In my opinion, putting an end to this waste of natural resources and efforts, and the generation of suffering and frustration for the projects undertaken by entrepreneurs who drag society under the deceitful policies of central banks is one of the great tasks of our time. And Bitcoin is posed as an alternative:

> The past instability of the market economy is the consequence of the exclusion of the most important regulator of the market mechanism, money, from itself being regulated by the market process. [...] the abolition of the government monopoly of the issue of money should involve also the disappearance of central banks as we know them.[15]

> *The Denationalization of Money*, Hayek

The Dead End

> Everything that can be broken must be broken; what will
> stand the blow will be good, and what will be
> pulverized, good for the trash.
>
> Dmitri Ivánovich Písarev on #Bitcoin

However, there are mechanisms by which the arrival of these
crises can be delayed, at the expense of snowballing the
situation—and the subsequent crisis even more serious, lasting,
and deeper—that is, by prolonging expansionary policies, the so-
called "stimulus plans." These plans have to grow in a
progressively accelerated manner to cover the first effect we
have discussed previously, the increase in the price of
production factors. If this does not happen, the above-mentioned
effects will be triggered, leading to the onset of the crisis. If the
economic agents discover this procedure and anticipate it by not
starting the projects with the monetary units that are "given" to
them, the economic crisis will also be triggered. If inflation
expectations are widely assumed, there will be an increase in the
prices of consumer goods and a significant increase in market
interest rates.

There are three possible triggers for these crises. First, that the
growth rate of credit expansion stops or slows down, that is,
"turning off the tap." If banks and authorities perceive the
possibility of a crisis and put on the brakes to prevent it from

becoming more serious, they will precipitate it. Next, if credit expansion is maintained but not at the pace necessary to cover the increase in the factors of production, it will expose the situation to the shrewdest entrepreneurs and they will drag the rest along, precipitating the crisis as well, in this case with high inflation and unemployment—*stagflation*. Finally, if the banking system maintains the rate of growth of credit expansion to cover the increase in the prices of the factors of production, there will be a generalized flight towards real values, a very significant increase in the prices of goods and services, and ultimately, the collapse of the monetary system in the event of hyperinflation, since the economic agents will look for other money. All this without avoiding the economic crisis, of course.

If you think there are signs of these scenarios, I don't blame you. Additionally, the pandemic has had two effects: First, it has accelerated credit expansion, since the demand for money, by economic agents and individuals to be able to face uncertainty, increased. But since it is for possible scenarios, they do not spend it, so generalized inflation is not perceived, which further accelerates credit expansion because "inflation" is not noticed. Secondly, there has been a significant contraction in production as a result of confinements and restrictions, that is, the supply of goods and services has been reduced considerably. A significant increase in money with a fall in the supply of goods and services inevitably leads to a rise in prices when the situation of uncertainty dissipates and these citizens start spending the money they hoarded on the goods and services available.

> The conclusion could not be clearer. Central banks have reached a real dead end. If they flee forward and push their policy of monetary expansion and monetization of an ever-increasing public deficit even further, they run the risk of generating a serious public debt and inflation crisis. But if in fear of moving from the 'Japanization' scenario prior to the

pandemic to a scenario close to 'Venezuelization' after it, they stop their ultra-loose monetary policy, then the overvaluation of the public debt markets will become immediately evident and a major financial crisis and economic recession, as painful as it is healthy in the medium and long term, will be generated. And it is in this context that the only sensible recommendation that can be given to investors is to sell all their fixed income positions as soon as possible, as it is not known how much longer the central banks will continue to artificially maintain such an exorbitant price of fixed income as has never been seen before in the history of mankind.[16]

The Economic Effects of the Pandemic, Herta de Soto

This time, if significant "inflation" is reached, there will be a way to protect against it. Let us remember that, for Hayek, a currency that was independent of the States would only have to solve the simplest problem: "to curb inflation."

Epilogue

The Future of Bitcoin

> In the face of danger, what saves is born.
>
> HÖDLerlin on #Bitcoin

I believe I have fulfilled the purpose I set out in the prologue: to have made it clear that two beliefs must recover their original nature as historical ideas: that a currency that is money must be backed by an authority, and that the "State" is a concept that can be applied to any political society and it is not possible to think of post-State political forms.

As for Bitcoin, it is in a process of discovery by the market— rarely in history have we witnessed such a monetization process—and when it is discovered, it will be seen that it solves problems of security, trust, and preservation, fundamental issues in a commodity as essential as money. Moreover, it fulfills in an unparalleled way the three laws that, for Hume, were fundamental for peaceful coexistence: that of the stability of possession, of its transference by consent, and of the performance of promises. However, an innovation of these characteristics will undoubtedly have a significant destructive effect, at the limit that of the State itself as a political form, but also, an expansive effect on trade and a new economy that requires a widely used global currency, so I believe that many business ideas will appear around it, forming a *cyber economy* that many States will take advantage of.

I also believe that it will continue to increase in value in the medium and long term, being acquired by large institutions and more people keeping their savings in it. Nothing suggests that States will stop *zombifying* the economy, so Bitcoin will continue to be an alternative in the coming years without abandoning its volatility, given that, with each wave of new users, there will continue to be ups and downs due to the fear of being left out when it rises and the fear that it will sink when it falls.

In the long run, however, Bitcoin will be a black hole that will absorb an enormous amount of value and produce a transfer of value of historic scope—and perhaps also a political transition—where the young, the tech savvy, and the curious will benefit. Bitcoin will have triumphed when states prefer to collect taxes on it rather than on the currencies they issue.

Nor should we forget that the situation of banking is delicate, with hardly any profitability, with a high concentration and dependence on the States, with a lousy image throughout the length and breadth of societies. Bitcoin is an alternative for everyone, both the young and not so young, a way to say no to the lack of privacy, no to the state monopoly of currency issuance, no to depending on third parties to access their funds, no to inflation, no to confiscatory taxes, no to debt in my name, no to bank bailouts, no to bank freezes, no to corruption with our money, no to the privileges of banking, no to political waste.

The future is not something to wait for, but something to build. That is what should invite us to take the reins and assume the personal commitment to try to build the best future we can, each one of us, with the tools we have at our disposal. Societies evolve by the strong determination of a minority of people who are capable of making a difference. In the coming years, we will see their expectations converge in the best monetary good.

You can avoid reality, but you cannot avoid the consequences of avoiding reality.

Ayn Rand on #Bitcoin

The State at a Crossroads

> Socrates: No man can escape fate, and therefore he is not fond of life and considers in what way he can best spend his appointed term.
>
> *Georgias*, Plato on #Bitcoin

After taking over the authority, political power has reached previously unimagined heights of influence. However, intoxicated by so much power, politicians abandoned their function of governing people and focused on the administration of things. By taking on a task that is not theirs and deviating from their role, their crisis may endanger the very idea of political community. This is why I consider it fundamental to think about new political forms and not to abandon ourselves to anarchy and individualism. "Ruler" comes from the Greek *Kybernetes*, meaning helmsman, so it is not surprising that the abandonment of its functions of directing people is leading our societies to shipwreck and every man for himself. It is in our hands to take the helm again.

A State locked in its labyrinth will have to reformulate itself to make way for another historical formula, while it loses competences, it is considered indispensable, it has difficulties in maintaining its central banks and struggles in competition with other States in the same situation. Once the veil of belief is removed and it reveals itself as a historical idea, its authority will be seriously questioned. Without another authority to counterbalance it, the State will only be violence.

Undoubtedly, Bitcoin has inflicted a very deep wound, the loss of the exclusive right to issue currency, something that affects in one way or another all-political life. We will see if it is a deadly wound for that form of despotism denounced by Tocqueville:

> I seek to trace the novel features under which despotism may appear in the world. The first thing that strikes the observation is an innumerable multitude of men all equal and alike, incessantly endeavoring to procure the petty and paltry pleasures with which they glut their lives. Each of them, living apart, is as a stranger to the fate of all the rest —his children and his private friends constitute to him the whole of mankind; as for the rest of his fellow-citizens, he is close to them, but he sees them not—he touches them, but he feels them not; he exists but in himself and for himself alone; and if his kindred still remains to him, he may be said at any rate to have lost his country.

> Above this race of men stands an immense and tutelary power, which takes upon itself alone to secure their gratifications, and to watch over their fate. That power is absolute, minute, regular, provident, and mild. It would be like the authority of a parent, if, like that authority, its object was to prepare men for manhood; but it seeks on the contrary to keep them in perpetual childhood: it is well content that the people should rejoice, provided they think of nothing but rejoicing. For their happiness such a government willingly labors, but it chooses to be the sole agent and the only arbiter of that happiness: it provides for their security, foresees and supplies their necessities, facilitates their pleasures, manages their principal concerns, directs their industry, regulates the descent of property, and subdivides their inheritances—what remains, but to spare them all the care of thinking and all the trouble of living?

Thus, it every day renders the exercise of the free agency of man less useful and less frequent; it circumscribes the will within a narrower range, and gradually robs a man of all the uses of himself. The principle of equality has prepared men for these things: it has predisposed men to endure them, and oftentimes to look on them as benefits.

After having thus successively taken each member of the community in its powerful grasp, and fashioned them at will, the supreme power then extends its arm over the whole community. It covers the surface of society with a network of small complicated rules, minute and uniform, through which the most original minds and the most energetic characters cannot penetrate, to rise above the crowd. The will of man is not shattered, but softened, bent, and guided: men are seldom forced by it to act, but they are constantly restrained from acting: such a power does not destroy, but it prevents existence; it does not tyrannize, but it compresses, enervates, extinguishes, and stupefies a people, till each nation is reduced to be nothing better than a flock of timid and industrious animals, of which the government is the shepherd.[17]

—Madrid, Spain, May 23, 2021, Álvaro D. María

About the Author

Álvaro D. María holds double degrees in law and philosophy and a Masters Program qualification in auditing and superior accounting. While working as an auditor, he wrote this book, his first. It was an instant success.

Shortly after it was published in Spanish in early 2022, he quit his auditing job to focus on interviews, podcasts, and speaking engagements at conferences and Bitcoin congresses worldwide, including LABITCONF (Argentina) and WOBitcoin (Spain), as well as teaching at the university level. He also started a Bitcoin consulting company. (https://btcconsulting360.com/).

Currently Álvaro is working with Gabriel Kurman on building the IFEB, Instituto de Filosofía y Economía de Bitcoin (Iberoamericano). He publishes monthly on Bitcoin, economics, politics, and philosophy for the Instituto Juan de Mariana (https://juandemariana.org/author/alvarodmaria).

This book marks the debut of *The Philosophy of Bitcoin* in English.

Acknowledgments

To Miraggio, for the artwork that serves as the cover of the book and to David, Manuel, Sergio, and Rafa for reviewing the book and for their friendship; as well as to those who trusted from the beginning, especially Coni, Ignacio, José Antonio, and Julia.

I also have to thank Manuel, Emérito, Adolfo, and Miguel for their work in spreading the knowledge they have about Bitcoin and without which this book would not have been possible, as well as Nick Szabo for his contributions.

Special thanks to Lunaticoin and Gabriel Kurman for helping make this book a reality.

"The Immaculate never fails."

Bitcoin: bc1qht7z25jsg75ylnrw264ep2nkp3pe6sh0q3qg24

Author of the Cover Artwork:
arte.miraggio@gmail.com
@MiraggioArte

Book author:
alvarodmaria@gmail.com
@Alvaro_DMaria
https://www.linkedin.com/in/alvarodmaria

Endnotes

---

[1]Perry Barlow, J. (n.d.) "Declaration of the Independence of Cyberspace," https://www.eff.org/cyberspace-independence.

[2] Zweig, S. (1964). *The World of Yesterday. An Autobiography*, 3-4.

[3] Parise, N. (2005). *El origen de la moneda. Signos pre-monetarios y formas arcaicas del intercambio*, ed. Bellaterra, 114.

[4] Hayek, F. A. (1990). *The Denationalisation of Money*. The Institute of Economic Affairs, 30-33.

[5] Polavieja, M. (n.d.). "El uso y abuso del término 'blockchain'" https://juandemariana.org/ijm-actualidad/analisis-diario/el-uso-y-abuso-del-termino-blockchain/

[6] Quintana, E. [@fosodefensivo] (2020, November 16). https://twitter.com/foso_defensivo/status/1328124004104802305

[7] Mahmudov, M. (n.d.). "The Ultimate Bitcoin Argument," https://medium.com/@apompliano/murad-mahmudov-the-ultimate-bitcoin-argument-b205a1987408

[8] Schmitt, C. (1934). *Teoría de la Constitución*, traducción de Francisco Ayala, Editorial Revista de derecho privado, 55-56.

[9] Bodin, J. (1967). *Six Books of the Commonwealth, 28.*

[10] Voegelin, E. (2000). *Political Religions*. Translated by Virginia Ann Schildjauer. University of Missouri Press, 29-30.

[11] Ortega y Gasset, J. (1930). *The Revolt of the Mases*. WW Norton & Co, 85-86.

[12] Mahmudov, M. (n.d.). "The Ultimate Bitcoin Argument," https://medium.com/@apompliano/murad-mahmudov-the-ultimate-bitcoin-argument-b205a1987408.

[13] Burke, E. (1790). *Reflections on the Revolution in France*. Oxford World's Classics, 127.

[14] Huerta de Soto, J. (2016). *Dinero, crédito bancario y ciclos económicos*, 6nd ed., Unión Editorial, Chapters V y VI.

[15] Hayek, F. A. (1990), *The Denationalisation of Money*. The Institute of Economic Affairs, 102.

[16] Huerta de Soto, J. (2021). "Los efectos económicos de la pandemia: Un análisis austriaco," *Cuadernos Para El Avance De La Libertad* 9, no. 2: 23.

[17] De Tocqueville, A. (2002). *Democracy in America*. Translated by Henry Reeve, 770–771.

Made in the USA
Monee, IL
04 September 2023

99a87de7-d67f-4cc8-ad88-c8d0388e2a0dR01